Contemporary Porridge Cookbook

Endless Porridge Possibilities

By

Angel Burns

© 2019 Angel Burns, All Rights Reserved.

License Notices

This book or parts thereof might not be reproduced in any format for personal or commercial use without the written permission of the author. Possession and distribution of this book by any means without said permission is prohibited by law.

All content is for entertainment purposes and the author accepts no responsibility for any damages, commercially or personally, caused by following the content.

Get Your Daily Deals Here!

Free books on me! Subscribe now to receive free and discounted books directly to your email. This means you will always have choices of your next book from the comfort of your own home and a reminder email will pop up a few days beforehand, so you never miss out! Every day, free books will make their way into your inbox and all you need to do is choose what you want.

What could be better than that?

Fill out the box below to get started on this amazing offer and start receiving your daily deals right away!

https://angel-burns.gr8.com

Table of Contents

Delicious Porridge Recipes 7

Recipe 1: Classic Scottish Porridge 8

Recipe 2: Quinoa and Berry Compote Porridge 10

Recipe 3: Apple and Pear Amaranth Porridge 13

Recipe 4: The Ultimate Chocolate Porridge 16

Recipe 5: Carrot Cake Porridge 18

Recipe 6: Fruity Polenta Porridge 21

Recipe 7: Coconut Buckwheat Porridge 24

Recipe 8: Raspberry and Dark Chocolate Porridge 27

Recipe 9: Almond and Fried Banana Porridge 29

Recipe 10: Vanilla Black Currant Porridge 33

Recipe 11: Norwegian Porridge 35

Recipe 12: Energizing Cacao Porridge 38

Recipe 13: Tahini Oat Porridge 40

Recipe 14: Whipped Berry Porridge 42

Recipe 15: Chai Brown Rice Porridge 45

Recipe 16: Gingery Cardamom Buckwheat Porridge ... 47

Recipe 17: Honey Japanese Rice Porridge 50

Recipe 18: Apple Maple Porridge 52

Recipe 19: Pistachio and Blueberry Porridge 54

Recipe 20: Poached Apricots Oat Porridge 56

Recipe 21: Turmeric Persimmon Porridge 59

Recipe 22: Whipped Chocolate Quinoa Porridge 62

Recipe 23: Rhubarb Oat Porridge 65

Recipe 24: Overnight Espresso Porridge 67

Recipe 25: Chocolate, Banana, and PB Porridge 70

Recipe 26: Baked Berry Porridge 72

Recipe 27: Pumpkin Pie Porridge 75

Recipe 28: Passionfruit Porridge topped with Blood Oranges 77

Recipe 29: Green Banana Porridge 80

Recipe 30: Gingerbread Porridge 83

Recipe 31: Almond Blackberry Porridge 85

Recipe 32: Chocolate Lentil Porridge 87

Recipe 33: Copenhagen Porridge 90

Recipe 34: Jamaican Corn Porridge 93

Recipe 35: Beetroot Cake Porridge 96

Recipe 36: Banana Porridge with Warm Berries 98

Recipe 37: Cinnamon Flax Porridge 101

Recipe 38: Honey and Walnut Porridge 103

Recipe 39: Toasted Coconut Porridge 105

Recipe 40: Barley Porridge with Apples and Raisins . 108

About the Author 111

Author's Afterthoughts 113

Delicious Porridge Recipes

HHHHHHHHHHHHHHHHHHHHHHHHHHHHHHHHHH

Recipe 1: Classic Scottish Porridge

Tasty, nutritious, packed with fiber, this classic Scottish oatmeal will fill you up in an instant. The ingredients may be simple, but the preparation method is authentic in Scotland and makes all the difference.

Yield: 2

Preparation Time: 35 minutes

Ingredient List:

- 1 ½ cup Pinhead Oatmeal
- 1 ½ cups Milk
- 2 cups Water
- Pinch of Salt

HHHHHHHHHHHHHHHHHHHHHHHHHHHHHHHHHH

Instructions:

Pour the water into a heavy saucepan.

Bring to a boil over the medium heat.

Sprinkle the oats over and stir to combine.

Bring the mixture to a boil again, continuously stirring with a wooden spoon.

Reduce to low and cover the saucepan. Let simmer for 25 minutes.

Halfway through, stir the salt into the oatmeal.

Make sure to stir every few minutes to get rid of the lumps.

Top as desired and serve. Enjoy!

Recipe 2: Quinoa and Berry Compote Porridge

Quinoa porridge made with homemade blueberry compote from scratch. This recipe may see like an overwhelming cooking process, but it is actually really simple to master. Garnish with fresh blueberries.

Yield: 2

Preparation Time: 10 minutes

Ingredient List:

- ½ cup Quinoa
- 1 tablespoon Maple Syrup
- 1 tablespoon Coconut Oil
- ½ teaspoons Vanilla Extract
- 1 cup Fresh Blueberries
- ½ cup plus 2 tablespoons Water
- 2 cups Milk
- 1 teaspoon Sugar
- Pinch of Salt

HHHHHHHHHHHHHHHHHHHHHHHHHHHHHHHHHHH

Instructions:

Toast the quinoa with the coconut oil in a saucepan over medium heat.

Pour ½ cup of water, milk, and stir in the salt.

Bring the mixture to a boil.

Drop to simmer and cook for 20 minutes.

Meanwhile, combine the blueberries, water, and sugar, in another saucepan over medium heat.

Cook for 5 minutes and stir in the vanilla.

Remove the quinoa from the heat and stir in the maple syrup.

Top with the blueberry compote.

Serve and enjoy!

Recipe 3: Apple and Pear Amaranth Porridge

Amaranth is combined with stewed apples and pears flavored with aromatic cinnamon. Bursting with flavors, this morning treat will energize you in a split second. Add some whipped cream to it if you like.

Yield: 1

Preparation Time: 30 minutes

Ingredient List:

- ¼ cup Amaranth
- ¾ cup Water
- ¼ cup diced Pear
- ¼ cup diced Apple
- 1 tablespoon Cinnamon
- 1 tablespoon Maple Syrup
- ½ cup Almond Milk

HHHHHHHHHHHHHHHHHHHHHHHHHHHHHHHH

Instructions:

Place the water and milk in a saucepan and bring to a boil over medium heat.

Add amaranth and lower the heat.

Simmer for 20 minutes.

Meanwhile, place the fruits, cinnamon, and maple syrup, in another saucepan over medium heat.

Stir to combine and cook for about 10 minutes, until the apples and pears become soft.

Transfer the amaranth to a bowl and top with the stewed fruits.

Enjoy!

Recipe 4: The Ultimate Chocolate Porridge

If you believe that dessert makes a great breakfast, then you will love the fact that you can have a creamy chocolate breakfast. Slices some strawberries on top for a more appealing look.

Yield: 4

Preparation Time: 10 minutes

Ingredient List:

- 2 cups Oats
- 4 tablespoons Maple Syrup
- 1 teaspoon Vanilla Extract
- 4 cups Milk
- 3 tablespoons Cacao Powder
- 4 tablespoons Chocolate Chips
- 4 tablespoons grated Chocolate

Instructions:

Combine the oats and milk in a saucepan.

Cook over medium heat for 5 minutes.

Stir in the cacao powder, grated chocolate, vanilla, and maple syrup.

Divide between 4 bowls.

Top with a tablespoon of chocolate chips.

Enjoy!

Recipe 5: Carrot Cake Porridge

Love eating carrot cake? Enjoy a yummy oatmeal for breakfast? Look no more because this recipe combines your two favorite dishes and creates one mouthwatering bowl of porridge.

Yield: 1

Preparation Time: 15 minutes

Ingredient List:

- 1 teaspoon Vanilla
- ½ cup Rolled Oats
- ¼ teaspoons Nutmeg
- ¼ teaspoons Cinnamon
- 1 Carrot, grated
- ½ cup Milk
- ½ cup Water
- 2 teaspoons ground Flaxseed
- 2 teaspoons Stevia or Sugar

HHHHHHHHHHHHHHHHHHHHHHHHHHHHHHHHH

Instructions:

Place everything in a saucepan and give it a good stir to combine.

Place the saucepan over medium heat and bring the mixture to a boil.

Reduce to simmer and cook for 7-10 minutes, stirring occasionally.

If needed, add a little bit more milk (or water).

Transfer to a bowl.

Enjoy!

Recipe 6: Fruity Polenta Porridge

Topped with figs, raspberries and a little bit of granola for texture, this coconut polenta porridge makes one hell of breakfast. Use different types of fruits if you prefer. It will be delicious either way.

Yield: 2

Preparation Time: 10 minutes

Ingredient List:

- ½ cup Polenta
- 1 ¼ cup Coconut Milk
- 2 cups Water
- 4 Figs, quartered
- 1/2 Raspberries
- 2 tablespoons Maple Syrup

HHHHHHHHHHHHHHHHHHHHHHHHHHHHHHHHH

Instructions:

Combine the milk and water in a bowl.

Add polenta to a saucepan and place 3 cups of the coconut water mixture.

Bring to a boil over medium heat.

Reduce to very low heat and cook until it gets too thick.

Then, stir in the remaining milky water.

Stir in the maple syrup.

Divide between 2 bowls.

Top with the fruits.

Enjoy!

Recipe 7: Coconut Buckwheat Porridge

Made the night before, this coconut and buckwheat porridge with chia seeds and vanilla is the most foolproof bowl of breakfast you will ever taste. Top with favorite toppings or enjoy it on its own.

Yield: 4

Preparation Time: 8 hours and 10 minutes

Ingredient List:

- 1 cup Buckwheat
- 3 cups Coconut Flakes, unsweetened
- 2 teaspoons Vanilla Extracts
- ¼ teaspoons Cinnamon
- 1 cup Water
- Pinch of Sea Salt

Instructions:

Place all of the ingredients in a large bowl.

Stir to combine and cover with a plastic wrap.

Place in the fridge and let the mixture sit overnight.

In the morning, transfer the mixture to a saucepan.

Place over medium heat and bring to a boil.

Reduce the heat and cook for 8 minutes. Make sure to stir occasionally.

Divide among 4 bowls and top with toppings, if desired.

Enjoy!

Recipe 8: Raspberry and Dark Chocolate Porridge

Dark chocolate and raspberries are a pair that never lets us down. Whether in desserts or in lovely breakfast porridges, this combination surely pleases everyone.

Yield: 2

Preparation Time: 10 minutes

Ingredient List:

- 1/3 cup Quinoa
- 1 tablespoon Chocolate Protein Powder
- 1/3 cup Quinoa Flakes
- 1 tablespoon Chocolate Green Powder
- ¼ cup Frozen Raspberries
- 2 tablespoons Chia Seeds
- 1 tablespoon Cacao Powder
- 1 tablespoon Maple Syrup
- 1 ½ cups Milk

HHHHHHHHHHHHHHHHHHHHHHHHHHHHHHHHHH

Instructions:

Place everything but the raspberries, in a mason jar.

Stir to combine well and sea.

Place in the fridge for 60 minutes.

Divide between two bowls.

Crumble the raspberries and place on top. Enjoy!

Recipe 9: Almond and Fried Banana Porridge

Looking for a fancy way to start your day? Well, this porridge has it all. Fried bananas, chopped almonds, oats, almond butter, hemp hearts, and maple syrup. Pretty irresistible, right?

Yield: 2

Preparation Time: 30 minutes

Ingredient List:

- ¼ cup chopped Almonds
- 2 cups Almond Milk
- ½ cup Steel Cut Oats
- 2 small Bananas
- 2 teaspoons Hemp Hearts
- 2 tablespoons Maple Syrup
- 1 tablespoon Coconut Oil
- 1/8 teaspoons Cinnamon
- 1 teaspoon Coconut Sugar
- 2 tablespoons Almond Butter
- Pinch of Sea Salt

HHHHHHHHHHHHHHHHHHHHHHHHHHHHHHHHH

Instructions:

Place the oats in a saucepan and over medium heat.

Cook for about 3 minutes, or until nutty and toasted.

Pour the milk over and stir in the salt.

Bring the mixture to a boil.

Reduce to simmer. Cook for 20 minutes, stirring occasionally.

In a skillet, melt the coconut oil over medium heat.

Add cinnamon and sugar.

Cut the bananas in half (lengthwise), and place them in the skillet with the cut side down.

Fry for a minute on each side. Transfer to a plate.

Add the almonds and cook until toasted.

Divide the porridge between 2 bowls and top with the bananas.

Sprinkle the almonds and hem hearts on top.

Drizzle with almond butter and maple syrup.

Serve and enjoy!

Recipe 10: Vanilla Black Currant Porridge

Gluten-free, rich in flavor, and most importantly super healthy and delicious, this porridge is the perfect way to start your day. You can substitute the red currants with blackberries or blueberries if you like.

Yield: 2

Preparation Time: 25 minutes

Ingredient List:

- ¾ cup Red Currants
- 1 teaspoon Pure Vanilla Extract
- ¾ cup Coconut Milk
- ½ cup Water
- ½ cup Buckwheat
- 2 teaspoons Honey

HHHHHHHHHHHHHHHHHHHHHHHHHHHHHHHH

Instructions:

Combine the water and buckwheat in a saucepan.

Cook for 5 minutes, or until absorbed.

Stir in the remaining ingredients.

Simmer for 15 minutes, but do not bring to a boil.

Serve as desired.

Enjoy!

Recipe 11: Norwegian Porridge

Creamy, rich, and both salty and sweet at the same time, this Norwegian porridge topped with dried cranberries and cinnamon will win your hearts in an instant.

Yield: 3

Preparation Time: 65 minutes

Ingredient List:

- 1 ½ cups Water
- 1 teaspoon Salt
- 1 tablespoon Honey
- 2 ½ cups Milk
- ¾ cup Rice
- 2 teaspoons Vanilla Extract
- 3/4 teaspoons Cinnamon
- 3 tablespoons dried Cranberries
- 1 tablespoon Butter
- 1 tablespoon Sugar

HHHHHHHHHHHHHHHHHHHHHHHHHHHHHHHHHH

Instructions:

Combine the rice and water in a saucepan over medium heat.

Bring to a boil, then reduce, and simmer for 10 minutes.

Add about a third of the milk, cover, and cook until it thickens.

Keep adding a little bit of the milk every 5 minutes until you use it all. The cooking shouldnt take loner than 50 minutes.

Stir in the sugar, butter, vanill, salt, and honey.

Divide among 3 bowls.

Sprinkle with cinnamon and top with dried cranberries.

Serve and enjoy!

Recipe 12: Energizing Cacao Porridge

If you are looking for something to kick you out of the house in the morning, then this is definitely it. An energizing cacao porridge with a secret energizing ingredient – guarana powder.

Yield: 1

Preparation Time: 10 minutes

Ingredient List:

- 1/3 cup Rolled Oats
- 2 tablespoons Cacao Powder
- ½ teaspoons Guarana Powder
- 2/3 cup Milk
- 1 tablespoon Maple Syrup
- 1 tablespoon Activated Buckwheat

Instructions:

Place everything but the activated buckwheat, in a saucepan.

Stir to combine.

Heat the mixture to a simmer and cook for 5 minutes.

Remove from heat and stir in the activated buckwheat.

Serve topped with fresh fruit.

Enjoy!

Recipe 13: Tahini Oat Porridge

Extremely delicious, gluten-free, and ready in just under 10 minutes, this tahini oatmeal with chopped almonds is the perfect way to start your day. Transfer to a plastic cup and take your breakfast with you.

Yield: 4

Preparation Time: 10 minutes

Ingredient List:

- 5 ½ ounces Oats
- 2 tablespoons Tahini
- 4 cups Milk
- 4 teaspoons Honey
- 4 tablespoons chopped Almonds

HHHHHHHHHHHHHHHHHHHHHHHHHHHHHHHHH

Instructions:

Combine the milk, oats, and tahini, in a saucepan over medium heat.

Bring the mixture to a boil, reduce the heat, and cook for 5 minutes.

Transfer to 4 bowls.

Drizzle with honey and top with chopped almonds.

Sere and enjoy!

Recipe 14: Whipped Berry Porridge

The mixed berries in this recipe give this porridge super powerful detoxifying properties that your body will be thankful for. You can use either fresh or frozen berries.

Yield: 2

Preparation Time: 12 minutes

Ingredient List:

- 1 cup Rolled Oats
- 1 cup mixed Berries
- 1 cup Almond Milk
- 3 teaspoons Honey
- 1 tablespoon Chia Seeds
- 1 tablespoon chopped Nuts
- 1 Peach, sliced

HHHHHHHHHHHHHHHHHHHHHHHHHHHHHHHHHHH

Instructions:

Combine the milk and oats in a saucepan.

Bring the mixture to a boil over medium heat.

Lower the heat and cook for 5 minutes.

Transfer it into a blender.

Add the berries and honey and blend until smooth.

Divide between the bowls.

Top with sliced peach, chia seeds, and nuts.

Enjoy!

Recipe 15: Chai Brown Rice Porridge

If you are into aromatic breakfasts, you will absolutely adore this recipe. A rich and creamy porridge filled with the most amazing chai flavors and aromas. This one is definitely a keeper.

Yield:

Preparation Time: 10 minutes

Ingredient List:

- 1 cup cooked Brown Rice
- 1 Vanilla Bean, split with the seeds scraped
- 1 Cinnamon Stick
- 1 cup Milk
- 1 slice of Ginger
- 1 teaspoon ground Flaxseed
- 2 teaspoons Honey

HHHHHHHHHHHHHHHHHHHHHHHHHHHHHHHH

Instructions:

In a saucepan, combine the rice, milk, vanilla, ginger, and cinnamon.

Place over medium heat and heat for a few minutes. Do not bring to a boil.

Divide between two bowls.

Top with flaxseed and drizzle with honey.

Enjoy!

Recipe 16: Gingery Cardamom Buckwheat Porridge

Ginger, cardamom, maple syrup, flaxseed, apple, and almond milk, accompany buckwheat and together create the most perfect bowl of breakfast porridge ever. Serve drizzled with honey yogurt.

Yield: 4

Preparation Time: 25 minutes

Ingredient List:

- 1 cup Buckwheat, soaked overnight and drained
- ½ teaspoons Nutmeg
- 1 ¼ inches of Ginger, grated
- 2 tablespoons Flaxseed
- ½ teaspoons Salt
- 2 ½ cups Almond Milk
- 1 teaspoon Cardamom
- 1 Apple, grated
- 2 tablespoons Maple Syrup
- 1 teaspoon Vanilla
- 2 tablespoons Coconut Oil
- Dried Berries, for serving

Instructions:

Combine the milk and salt in a saucepan.

Bring to a boil over medium heat and stir in the buckwheat.

Bring the mixture back to a boil, then reduce to simmer.

Stir in the coconut oil, vanilla, maple, cardamom, nutmeg, flaxseed, and ginger.

Let simmer for about 10 minutes.

Divide between bowls.

Top with berries.

Enjoy!

Recipe 17: Honey Japanese Rice Porridge

This authentic Japanese porridge made with Japanese-style rice, ginger, and honey, is all you need for breakfast. I recommend adding nothing but the ingredients in this recipe for the best flavor.

Yield: 4

Preparation Time: 70 minutes

Ingredient List:

- 1 cup uncooked Japanese-style white Rice
- 1 teaspoon Salt
- 4 tablespoons Honey
- 5 cups Water
- 1 tablespoon grated Ginger

HHHHHHHHHHHHHHHHHHHHHHHHHHHHHHHHH

Instructions:

Wash the rice and drain. Repeat until the water is no longer cloudy.

Place the rice in a heavy-bottomed saucepan and add the water.

Let the rice sit for 30 minutes.

Stir in salt and ginger and cover the saucepan.

Bring to a boil over medium heat, then drop to simmer, and cook for 30 minutes.

Let sit for a few minutes.

Serve drizzled with honey. Enjoy!

Recipe 18: Apple Maple Porridge

Maple syrup, cinnamon, and sultanas, give this delightful oatmeal a flavorful touch that is hard to resist. Packed with the most warming spices, this porridge will definitely kickstart your day.

Yield: 4

Preparation Time: 10 minutes

Ingredient List:

- 1 tablespoon Maple Syrup
- 1 tablespoon Sugar
- 4 ounces Oats
- 2 cups Milk
- 1 teaspoon Cinnamon
- 1 ½ ounces Sultanas
- Pinch of Salt

HHHHHHHHHHHHHHHHHHHHHHHHHHHHHHHHHH

Instructions:

In a saucepan, place all of the ingredients.

Stir to combine well.

Place over medium heat and bring to a boil.

Reduce to simmer and cook for a few minutes, until the liquid is mostly absorbed and the porridge is creamy, but thick.

Top with extra cinnamon if you want to.

Serve and enjoy!

Recipe 19: Pistachio and Blueberry Porridge

Crunchy pistachios and soft and sweet blueberries give this oat porridge an incredible texture. This recipe uses almond milk but any kind of milk will do just fine.

Yield: 1

Preparation Time: 10 minutes

Ingredient List:

- 3 ½ ounces Blueberries
- ¾ cup Almond Milk
- 1 tablespoon chopped Pistachios
- 1 Sachet 'Oats so Simple'
- Pinch of Cinnamon

Instructions:

Place half of the blueberries in a blender and blend until pureed.

Combine the oats, milk and cinnamon, in a microwave-safe bowl.

Place in the microwave and cook as stated on the package.

Add the pureed berries and stir to combine.

Top with pistachios and remaining blueberries.

Enjoy!

Recipe 20: Poached Apricots Oat Porridge

Who doesn't love poached fruits? Make them a topping for your morning porridge and you will pack yourself with the most wonderful feel-good vibes. This recipe uses apricots but peaches will be delightful too.

Yield: 2

Preparation Time: 10 minutes

Ingredient List:

- ¼ cup Almond Milk
- 5 ounces Oatmeal
- 4 tablespoons Honey
- 2 tablespoons Brown Sugar
- A Handful of dried Fruits
- Poached Apricots:
- 2 Apricots, pitted and halved
- 1 clove Vanilla Split
- ¼ cup Water
- 3 ½ ounces Sugar

Instructions:

Combine the oatmeal, milk, and brown sugar, in a saucepan over medium heat.

Bring to a boil, lower the heat, and let cook for about 8 minutes. Stir occasionally.

Meanwhile, combine all of the poached apricots ingredients in another saucepan.

Cook until the fruit softens and the liquid turns to syrup.

Divide the porridge between 2 bowls.

Top with poached apricots, dried fruit, and drizzle with honey.

Enjoy!

Recipe 21: Turmeric Persimmon Porridge

Warming, gingery, fruity, and creamy, this amazing turmeric persimmon porridge is packed with the most powerful antioxidant properties that will nourish you from the inside out.

Yield: 2

Preparation Time: 40 minutes

Ingredient List:

- 1 cup Rolled Oats
- 1 ½ teaspoons minced Ginger
- 2 medium Persimmons
- 4 tablespoons Flaxseed Meal
- 1 teaspoon Turmeric
- ½ teaspoons Cinnamon
- 1 cup Coconut Milk
- Pinch of Salt
- 2 tablespoons Honey

HHHHHHHHHHHHHHHHHHHHHHHHHHHHHHHHHH

Instructions:

Combine the persimmons, coconut milk, ginger, cinnamon, salt, and turmeric, in a blender.

Blend until smooth.

Divide the oats and flaxseed meal between two bowls.

Pour the blended mixture over.

Stir to combine.

Let sit for about 30 minutes in the fridge.

Drizzle with honey and enjoy!

Recipe 22: Whipped Chocolate Quinoa Porridge

Light and delightful, this fiber-loaded porridge with whipped chocolate oatmeal and crunchy quinoa topping will knock your socks off. The cacao makes this taste like a dessert.

Yield: 2

Preparation Time: 12 minutes

Ingredient List:

- ½ cup Oats
- 1 cup Water
- 2/3 cup Almond Milk
- 2 teaspoons Honey
- 2 teaspoons Coconut Oil
- 1 tablespoon Cacao Powder
- A pinch of Salt
- Crunchy Quinoa:
- ¼ cup Flaxseeds, crushed
- 1 teaspoon Coconut Sugar
- ¼ cup Almonds, crushed
- ¼ cup Sunflower Seeds
- ¼ cup Cashews, crushed
- 1 teaspoon Coconut Oil
- ½ cup Quinoa
- A pinch of Sea Salt

HHHHHHHHHHHHHHHHHHHHHHHHHHHHHHHHHHH

Instructions:

Combine the water and oats in a saucepan and place over medium heat.

Bring to a boil, reduce the temperature, and cook for 5 minutes.

Meanwhile, melt the coconut oil for the quinoa in a skillet, then, add all of the remaining quinoa ingredients. Toast for about 5 minutes.

Place the oatmeal in a blender.

Add the honey, almond milk, cacao powder, salt, and coconut oil.

Blend until smooth.

Divide between bowls.

Top with the crunchy quinoa mixture.

Enjoy!

Recipe 23: Rhubarb Oat Porridge

Rhubarb, orange juice, and oats, make one healthy, nutrient-packed, and extremely delightful bowl of porridge. Serve with your favorite toppings, but I suggest to keep it simple with some chopped nuts.

Yield: 2

Preparation Time: 12 minutes

Ingredient List:

- 1 ½ cup Milk
- ½ cup Orange Juice
- 1 cup chopped Rhubarb
- ½ teaspoons Cinnamon
- 2 teaspoons Honey

HHHHHHHHHHHHHHHHHHHHHHHHHHHHHHHHHHH

Instructions:

Combine everything, except the honey, in a saucepan.

Place over medium heat and bring to a boil.

Reduce the heat and cook until the rhubarb becomes tender, about 5 minutes.

Cover the saucepan and let sit off heat for 5 minutes.

Stir in the honey and serve.

Enjoy!

Recipe 24: Overnight Espresso Porridge

If you are looking for that morning kick, you will not find a better recipe than this one. Oat porridge with chia seeds and strong brewed coffee, this has to be the ultimate energizing breakfast.

Yield: 2

Preparation Time: 8 hours and 10 minutes

Ingredient List:

- 1 cup Rolled Oats
- ½ cup Strong Brewed Coffee
- 1 teaspoon Vanilla Extract
- 1 tablespoon Chia Seeds
- 2 tablespoons Maple Syrup
- ¾ cup Almond Milk

Instructions:

Place all of the ingredients in a bowl.

Stir to combine well.

Cover the bowl and place in the fridge. Let sit for a few hours or overnight.

In the morning, you can either serve the porridge cold straight from the fridge, or you can heat it on the stove for a few minutes.

Top with your favorite toppings and enjoy!

Recipe 25: Chocolate, Banana, and PB Porridge

Is there a lovelier combination than the one of chocolate, bananas, and peanut butter? This sweet and creamy buckwheat porridge will surely satisfy everyone. The lemon juice adds a touch of needed freshness.

Yield: 2

Preparation Time: 5 minutes

Ingredient List:

- ½ cup Buckwheat, soaked overnight and drained
- ½ teaspoons Vanilla
- 1 Banana
- ½ cup Milk
- 2 tablespoons Sunflower Seeds, soaked overnight and drained
- 1 teaspoon Cocoa Powder
- 3 small Dates
- 2 teaspoons Lemon Juice
- 2 tablespoons Peanut Butter

Instructions:

Place the banana, dates, buckwheat, lemon juice, vanilla, cocoa, and sunflower seeds in a blender.

Blend until really smooth.

Divide between 2 serving bowls.

Drizzle with peanut butter.

Enjoy!

Recipe 26: Baked Berry Porridge

Who says that porridge cannot be baked? Crunchy and with amazing texture, this berry-packed and cinnamon oat porridge surely has to be the best morning treat you have ever tried.

Yield: 4

Preparation Time: 35 minutes

Ingredient List:

- 5 ½ ounces Oats
- 1 pound mixed Berries
- 1 Egg
- 2 tablespoons Honey
- 1 ¼ cup Milk
- ½ teaspoons Cinnamon
- 4 tablespoons Honey Yogurt

Instructions:

Preheat your oven to 350 degrees F.

Combine the oats and cinnamon in a bowl.

Whisk together the egg, milk, and honey.

In a baking dish, place half of the berries.

Layer the oats on top.

Pour the milk mixture over.

Top with the remaining berries.

Bake for about 25 minutes.

Serve drizzled with honey yogurt.

Enjoy!

Recipe 27: Pumpkin Pie Porridge

Ready in 5 minutes, this foolproof pumpkin porridge with oats is the perfect way to make picky kids eat pumpkin. Serve topped with whipped cream for an added sweetness.

Yield: 2

Preparation Time: 10 minutes

Ingredient List:

- ½ cup Oats
- 1 cup Milk
- 1/3 cup Pumpkin Puree
- 2 teaspoons Honey
- ½ teaspoons Pumpkin Pie Spice
- 2 teaspoons ground Walnuts

HHHHHHHHHHHHHHHHHHHHHHHHHHHHHHHHH

Instructions:

Place all of the ingredients, except walnuts, in a saucepan over medium heat.

Stir well to combine and bring the mixture to a boil.

Lower it to simmer and cook for 5 minutes.

Divide between two bowls.

Sprinkle with ground walnuts and serve.

Enjoy!

Recipe 28: Passionfruit Porridge topped with Blood Oranges

The recipe name says it all. Sweet and delicious porridge with oats and passionfruit topped with refreshing blood oranges for a tangy kick. Serve drizzled with honey if desired.

Yield: 2

Preparation Time: 8 hours and 10 minutes

Ingredient List:

- 1 cup Oats
- 2 Blood Oranges, peeled and sliced
- 2 Passionfruits, flesh only
- 1 tablespoon Chia Seeds
- 2 teaspoons Maple Syrup
- 2 teaspoons Buckwheat
- 4 teaspoons Coconut Flakes
- 2 teaspoons Hemp Hearts
- 2 cups Almond Milk
- Pinch of Salt

HHHHHHHHHHHHHHHHHHHHHHHHHHHHHHHH

Instructions:

Combine oats, milk, chia seeds, maple syrup, and salt, in a large bowl.

Cover and let sit in the fridge overnight.

In the morning, add the passionfruit and stir to combine everything well.

Divide between two bowls.

Arrange the blood orange slices on top.

Sprinkle with the remaining ingredients.

Serve and enjoy!

Recipe 29: Green Banana Porridge

This Caribbean delight will bring the exotic flavors to your kitchen. So, sweet, creamy, and super aromatic, this breakfast porridge made with green bananas and coconut milk is pure perfection.

Yield: 3-4

Preparation Time: 18 minutes

Ingredient List:

- 3 Green Bananas
- 1 teaspoon Vanilla Extract
- 2 ½ cups Water
- 2 cups Coconut Milk
- 1/3 cup Condensed Coconut Milk
- ¼ teaspoons Cinnamon
- ¼ teaspoons Nutmeg
- Pinch of Salt

HHHHHHHHHHHHHHHHHHHHHHHHHHHHHHHHH

Instructions:

Remove the debris from the bananas and peel.

Place in a blender along with the water.

Blend until smooth.

Transfer to a saucepan and bring to a boil over medium heat.

Stir in the coconut milk, cinnamon, salt, and nutmeg.

Add the condensed coconut milk and bring to a boil again.

Simmer for 5 minutes.

Divide between bowls and enjoy!

Recipe 30: Gingerbread Porridge

Grain-free, paleo, and super sweet, this morning treat is the perfect breakfast for the chili winter mornings. Top with chopped nuts and honey for an even crunchier texture.

Yield: 1

Preparation Time: 10 minutes

Ingredient List:

- ½ cup Pecans
- 1/3 teaspoons Nutmeg
- ¼ teaspoons Cinnamon
- ¼ teaspoons ground Ginger
- ½ teaspoons Molasses
- 1 teaspoon Maple Syrup
- 2 tablespoons Flaxseeds
- ½ cup Almond Milk
- Pinch of Salt
- Pinch of Cloves
- 1 scoop Protein Collagen Peptides

HHHHHHHHHHHHHHHHHHHHHHHHHHHHHHHHH

Instructions:

Place the pecans in a food processor and pulse until ground.

Add flaxseeds and pulse again for a few more seconds.

Transfer to a bowl and place the remaining ingredients.

Stir to combine well.

Serve immediately and enjoy!

Recipe 31: Almond Blackberry Porridge

Almond flour and blackberries star in this simple but super delicious breakfast porridge. For a creamier texture, substitute the water with coconut milk. You can even add some coconut flakes on top.

Yield: 2

Preparation Time: 15 minutes

Ingredient List:

- 1 ½ cups Almond Flour
- 1 cup Blackberries
- 1 ½ cups Water
- 1 tablespoon Maple Syrup
- Pinch of Cinnamon
- Pinch of Salt

HHHHHHHHHHHHHHHHHHHHHHHHHHHHHHHH

Instructions:

In a saucepan, combine the water, salt, and almond flour.

Cook for 8 minutes, or until the mixture is thickened and begins to boil.

Stir in the maple syrup and divide between two bowls.

Top with blackberries.

Enjoy!

Recipe 32: Chocolate Lentil Porridge

Who says that you only have to use oats, grains, and seeds for your morning porridge? Make this recipe with red lentils, cacao powder, almond butter, cinnamon, and maple, and be mind-blown by its delightfulness.

Yield: 2

Preparation Time: 10 minutes

Ingredient List:

- 6 tablespoons dried Red Lentils, soaked overnight and drained
- 1 tablespoon Cinnamon
- 1 tablespoon Almond Butter
- 2 tablespoons Cacao Powder
- 1 tablespoon Flaxseed
- ½ cup Water
- ½ cup Milk
- 2 tablespoons Maple Syrup

Instructions:

Combine the lentils, water, and milk, in a saucepan.

Bring to a boil over medium heat.

Reduce to simmer and let cook for 10 minutes, stirring occasionally.

Stir in the remaining ingredients.

Divide between bowls.

Serve and enjoy!

Recipe 33: Copenhagen Porridge

Rich in some of the most amazing sweet flavors, this porridge in a Copenhagen style will not only fill your tummy in the morning, but it will also satisfy your sweet tooth in a jiffy.

Yield: 2

Preparation Time: 10 minutes

Ingredient List:

- ½ cup Rolled Oats
- 1 teaspoon Cinnamon
- ½ cup Coconut Milk
- ¼ cup Rze Flakes
- ½ cup rolled Spelt Flakes
- 1 tablespoon Dark Chocolate Shavings
- 2 tablespoons Maple Syrup
- 1 teaspoon Vanilla
- 3 tablespoons Dark Cocoa
- 1 teaspoon Cocoa Nibs
- A handful of Pomegranate Seeds
- Pinch of Salt
- 1 ½ cups Water
- ½ Apple, sliced

HHHHHHHHHHHHHHHHHHHHHHHHHHHHHHHHH

Instructions:

Place everything but the cocoa nibs, chocolate, pomegranate, and apple, in a saucepan.7

Bring the mixture to a boil.

Lower the heat and cook for 8 more minutes.

Divide between bowls and top with the remaining ingredients.

Enjoy!

Recipe 34: Jamaican Corn Porridge

Corn porridge or originally called hominy, this dish is a classic breakfast in Jamaica. Flavored with vanilla and cinnamon and made with coconut milk, this porridge is a crowd pleaser.

Yield: 4

Preparation Time: 40 minutes

Ingredient List:

- 2 cups Coconut Milk
- 2 cups Water
- ¼ teaspoons Salt
- 2 cups Hominy Corn
- 1 teaspoon Vanilla Extract
- 3 Cinnamon Leaves
- Pinch of Nutmeg
- 2 tablespoons Honey

HHHHHHHHHHHHHHHHHHHHHHHHHHHHHHHHHH

Instructions:

Pour 1 cup of water in a saucepan and add the cinnamon leaves.

Bring to a boil and cook for 2 minutes.

Add the corn and salt.

Lower the heat and cook until the water reduces.

Then, stir in the remaining water.

Again, cook until the water reduces.

Pour the coconut milk into the hominy and cook until the mixture thickens.

Stir in vanilla and nutmeg, and discard the cinnamon leaves.

Serve drizzled with honey.

Enjoy!

Recipe 35: Beetroot Cake Porridge

Oats, sultanas, vitamin-packed beets, chopped pecans, sugar, and honey. Do you really need a more powerful kick than that to get you started in the morning? Throw in some grated chocolate if you want to.

Yield: 1

Preparation Time: 10 minutes

Ingredient List:

- 1 cup Rolled Oats
- ½ cup grated Beetroot
- ¼ cup Sultanas
- 2 teaspoons Honey
- 1 teaspoon Brown Sugar
- 2 cups Water

HHHHHHHHHHHHHHHHHHHHHHHHHHHHHHHHHH

Instructions:

Place all of the ingredients, except the honey, in a saucepan and stir to combine.

Place over medium heat.

Cook for 5 minutes, until thickens.

Transfer to a bowl and drizzle with the honey.

Enjoy!

Recipe 36: Banana Porridge with Warm Berries

If you have a rumbling gut, this recipe name surely brings water to your mouth. But wait until you try it. You will be lickin your cereal bowl in no time. Warming and extremely delcious porridge.

Yield: 1

Preparation Time: 10 minutes

Ingredient List:

- ¾ cup Milk
- ½ cup Oats
- 1 small Banana
- 1 tablespoon Nut Butter
- 1 cup frozen Berries

HHHHHHHHHHHHHHHHHHHHHHHHHHHHHHHHHH

Instructions:

Mash the banana with a fork, in a cereal bowl.

Add the milk and oats and stir to combine.

Place in the microwave and heat for 1 minute.

Place the berries in a small bowl and microwave for 30-35 seconds.

Stir and then microwave for another 30 seconds.

Top the porridge with the berries and drizzle the butter over.

Enjoy!

Recipe 37: Cinnamon Flax Porridge

Ready in just 2 minutes in your microwave, this flaxseed porridge with coconut milk and cinnamon will blow you away. Great for those busy mornings.

Yield: 1

Preparation Time: 5 minutes

Ingredient List:

- 1/3 cup ground Flaxseed
- 1 cup Water
- ½ cup Coconut Milk
- ¼ teaspoons Cinnamon
- 1 teaspoon Brown Sugar

HHHHHHHHHHHHHHHHHHHHHHHHHHHHHHHH

Instructions:

Place all of the ingredients in a microwave-safe bowl.

Stir well to combine.

Place in the microwave and cook for 2 minutes on HIGH.

Serve and enjoy!

Recipe 38: Honey and Walnut Porridge

Sweet honey and walnut amaranth porridge. What could you possibly need more for breakfast? Creamy and crunchy at the same time, this morning treat will be enjoyed by everyone.

Yield: 4

Preparation Time: 30 minutes

Ingredient List:

- ½ teaspoons Salt
- 2 cups Amaranth
- 4 cups Water
- 4 tablespoons chopped Walnuts
- 4 tablespoons Honey

HHHHHHHHHHHHHHHHHHHHHHHHHHHHHHHHHH

Instructions:

Place the water and amaranth in a saucepan.

Give it a good stir and place over medium heat.

Bring to a boil.

Reduce to simmer and cook for about 20 minutes, or until the liquid is fully absorbed.

Divide among 4 serving bowls.

Drizzle with honey and top with walnuts.

Enjoy!

Recipe 39: Toasted Coconut Porridge

Quinoa and oats combined in a creamy and delicious mixture of toasted coconut flakes and coconut milk. A rich and delicious full coconut breakfast.

Yield: 4

Preparation Time: 20 minutes

Ingredient List:

- 1 ¼ cup Coconut Milk
- ½ cup Coconut Flakes
- ½ cup Quinoa
- 1 ½ cup Rolled Oats
- 1 cup Water
- ¼ teaspoons Cinnamon
- 4 tablespoons Honey
- A Pinch of Salt

HHHHHHHHHHHHHHHHHHHHHHHHHHHHHHHHHHH

Instructions:

Combine the quinoa, water, and salt, and bring to a boil over medium heat.

Reduce to simmer and cook for about 15 minutes.

Stir in the oats, milk, and cinnamon.

Cook for a few minutes.

Meanwhile, toast the coconut flakes in a nonstick skillet over medium heat.

Divide the porridges between bowls and top with toasted coconut.

Drizzle with a tablespoon of honey.

Enjoy!

Recipe 40: Barley Porridge with Apples and Raisins

Whole grain and healthy breakfast that vegans will adore. The touch of date syrup in this recipe makes all the difference so I recommend not to substitute it with another ingredient.

Yield: 2

Preparation Time: 30 minutes

Ingredient List:

- 10 Raisins
- ½ cup Barley
- 1 ½ cup Soy Milk
- 2 Walnuts, chopped finely
- 2 Apples, chopped
- 1 tablespoon Pumpkin Seeds
- 1 ½ cups Water
- ¼ teaspoons Cinnamon
- 1 tablespoon Date Syrup
- ¼ teaspoons Nutmeg

HHHHHHHHHHHHHHHHHHHHHHHHHHHHHHHHHH

Instructions:

Combine the Water and barley in a saucepan.

Place on the medium heat and bring to a boil.

Reduce the heat and cook for about 15 minutes. Make sure to stir occasionally.

Stir in the cinnamon, nutmeg, soy milk, and raisins.

Bring the mixture to a boil.

Turn off the heat and then stir in the date syrup.

Top with apple, walnuts, and pumpkin seeds.

Enjoy!

About the Author

Angel Burns learned to cook when she worked in the local seafood restaurant near her home in Hyannis Port in Massachusetts as a teenager. The head chef took Angel under his wing and taught the young woman the tricks of the trade for cooking seafood. The skills she had learned at a young age helped her get accepted into Boston University's Culinary Program where she also minored in business administration.

Summers off from school meant working at the same restaurant but when Angel's mentor and friend retired as head chef, she took over after graduation and created classic and new dishes that delighted the diners. The restaurant flourished under Angel's culinary creativity and one customer developed more than an appreciation for Angel's food. Several months after taking over the position, the young woman met her future husband at work and they have been inseparable ever since. They still live in Hyannis Port with their two children and a cocker spaniel named Buddy.

Angel Burns turned her passion for cooking and her business acumen into a thriving e-book business. She has authored several successful books on cooking different types of dishes using simple ingredients for novices and experienced chefs alike. She is still head chef in Hyannis Port and says she will probably never leave!

Author's Afterthoughts

With so many books out there to choose from, I want to thank you for choosing this one and taking precious time out of your life to buy and read my work. Readers like you are the reason I take such passion in creating these books.

It is with gratitude and humility that I express how honored I am to become a part of your life and I hope that you take the same pleasure in reading this book as I did in writing it.

Can I ask one small favour? I ask that you write an honest and open review on Amazon of what you thought of the book. This will help other readers make an informed choice on whether to buy this book.

My sincerest thanks,

Angel Burns

If you want to be the first to know about news, new books, events and giveaways, subscribe to my newsletter by clicking the link below

https://angel-burns.gr8.com

or Scan QR-code

Printed in Great Britain
by Amazon